"The Buoyant Business is a must read for any leader with change management responsibilities. With a solid framework and actionable advice, this book gives you the blueprint to examine your processes and build a new operating model based on simplicity, sustainability, and effectiveness. A true wake up call to streamline and eliminate existing redundancies, and drive your organization to operational success."

-Maria I. Piastre
President, Metallix

"The solution is simple, and this is exactly what companies need. This isn't just a book about change, it's about problem solving and transformation in the 'Deepest Waters' of any business. This book provides the tools and resources to make the complex simple, to give the flexibility and nimbleness businesses need to cope with modern times. This is the next best thing to being allowed to print your own money."

-Ed Coates
Director of Operations
ADM Group

"Adriana's passion and commitment to improving business and process shines through in *THE BUOYANT BUSINESS*, and the book accomplishes its goal of kickstarting the reader to take the next step. The focus on simplicity is both classically proven and ever timely given the disruption experiences many companies have undertaken."

Eric Matthias

Business Transformation Director | Lean Master Facilitator

"In this book, Adriana shares a treasure. With her talent to look for simple solutions and improve processes, she gives us resources, tools, and all we need to simplify the complex. It has been proven that if a company does not have good processes, it will not survive. *The Buoyant Business* will show you where to look to improve your process. This is the book to read if you want to be successful in your business."

Kathe Loaiza

Co-founder and CEO of Golab Cosmetics and Serial Entrepreneur

ADRIANA ROZO-ANGULO

THE BUOYANT BUSINESS

HOW SIMPLICITY CAN KEEP
YOUR ORGANIZATION AFLOAT IN
TODAY'S STORMY ECONOMY

THE BUOYANT BUSINESS

For more information visit:
Fig Factor Media, LLC. | www.figfactormedia.com
MAS-Connections | www.mas-connections.com

Cover Design by Juan Pablo Ruiz
Layout by Manuel Serna
Printed in the United States of America

ISBN: 978-1-952779-47-3

Library of Congress Control Number: 2021904905

FIG
FACTOR
MEDIA

To Miguel Angulo, my love, my friend, my support. Thank you for always encouraging me to be the best version of myself, for supporting all my ideas, and for standing beside me when I need you and giving me the space when I need it.

To Sebastian and Matthew, my reason to be better every day. My desire is to inspire you to find your purpose and dream big.

To God, thank you for closing the doors that needed to be closed and opening the many doors that took me to the path that I am on today. Thank you for your guidance and blessings.

TABLE OF CONTENTS

ACKNOWLEDGMENTS

I want to thank every person who impacted my life and helped me to forge my path on this journey. I am the result of the experiences, challenges, and people I encountered during these years. My way of seeing the world, life, and business is the direct result of those experiences and the influence that different people had on my life at every stage.

And most importantly, I want to thank God for revealing to me my purpose, placing before me the opportunities as well as the responsibilities, and for the talents and the relationships He has given me to do what He puts in my heart.

FOREWORD

Adriana Rozo-Angulo is one of those rare people that you meet with an incredible soul and glow to her. Ever since I had the wonderful pleasure of meeting and befriending Adriana a few months ago, she has had the idea of making an impact in the lives of others. I can see it in her eyes. I felt it in her energy. She is an expert in corporate systems and processes with decades of professional experience in the private sector, and she was excited about taking others on an enlightening journey, deep into the rich treasure trove of her mind for useful lessons for all of us.

Part of what inspired her to write this book is the ardent belief that processes exist both to simplify human lives and help companies grow. Her passion for these processes and change, as well as her need for a simple guide to the main concepts and information concerning decision making, change management, and business transformation, further motivated her to write this book.

Making the decision and taking the actions necessary to see this long-held dream of hers through to fruition, has been a real turning point in her life. Although Adriana has had the desire and impetus to do it, coming from a corporate background, she did not yet have the proper tools to effectively implement her ideas. All she needed was someone to come along and finally light the match to get her creative juices flowing. Oftentimes, extraordinary people with great potential like hers just need a little push, a little guidance, someone to show them a different path toward new horizons.

This is why I was so extremely humbled when she asked me to write the foreword to the incredible creation that is *The Buoyant Business*. Adriana has told me more than once that I changed her life, but in reality, all I did was serve as the catalyst to her own empowerment. Igniting the spark that was already yearning to burst into flames within her all along inspired her to go further and share with the world a little bit of the immense amount of wisdom she has.

In the coming pages, Adriana puts together a brief guide detailing invaluable information and concepts in a simple way that gives readers more clarity on the topics she discusses and elucidates what we should do and what our focus should be, now that we have entered into a novel business era. One of her main hopes in sharing her vast knowledge and experiences found in this primer is expediting the learning curve for entrepreneurs with ambitions to grow their companies.

I have had the honor of seeing first-hand how she has grown throughout this process and evolved by taking what I have taught her about branding and successfully harnessing the magic found within in each and every one of us to accomplish one of her enduring aspirations. It has been very emotional, magical, and incredible to witness. I am beyond excited, happy, and proud of her. I love seeing Adriana truly blossom and expand her wings, and it has been a true privilege to be a part of her magical journey.

Jaqueline S. Ruiz

24x Author, international Speaker, Serial Entrepreneur, and Pilot

INTRODUCTION

I have planned to write this book for many years. I changed the concept several times, but in the end, I came back to my original idea. What has driven me to write *"The Buoyant Business"* was my own need for a simple guide to the main concepts and information that I work with professionally every day.

During my time in the corporate world, I've had the opportunity to be involved in many steps of the command chain. For the last 20 years, I have been part of a team that makes important and radical decisions and changes. I have also been on the other side, with a group of employees who are told of the decisions and are expected to execute them.

This book contains my personal approach to decision making, change management, and business transformation.

I am passionate about process and change. I fervently believe that processes exist to facilitate our lives and help with company growth. I believe that each process must be simple enough to give the company the flexibility to adapt when changes occur, but at the same time should be robust enough to sustain the company in moments of disruption.

I used to be passionate about efficiency until I discovered that my understanding of efficiency was limited. In fluid times like the ones we are living in now, the concept of efficiency as we know it can be a disadvantage if it limits your agility.

With the fluid conditions of the market and the constant change in the world, some of the business models that we studied in school and used in our companies are not applicable anymore. We need a new word in the dictionary to express that situation that involves many factors—the need to be firm and robust but also fluid enough to react with agility.

I think of it as being *Buoyant.*

Water is the perfect example of the current business model—it can be calm one day, and the next day it can have high waves and riptides. It can also destroy everything in an instant. However, water may look rough on the surface, but it can be calm deep below.

This book shares my opinion—based on my education and experiences—on what we should do and what our focus should be now that a new business era is starting. Our business should be like a buoy that provides guidance, stays out on the water, bobbing up and down with the changing conditions, but never sinks.

I am excited to provide you with this quick guide containing information and concepts written in a simple way that can help you clarify something or give you a topic of conversation. I am sure that you will want to keep it at your desk.

It is also my hope that this book can be useful for entrepreneurs with aspirations to grow their companies. I am sharing my knowledge and experiences to expedite the learning curve. I believe that entrepreneurs who establish processes will be liberated, allowing them to work on the vision they have for their company instead of performing everyday activities and tasks.

Chapter 1

———

OUR BRAIN CONTROLS OUR RESPONSE TO CHANGE

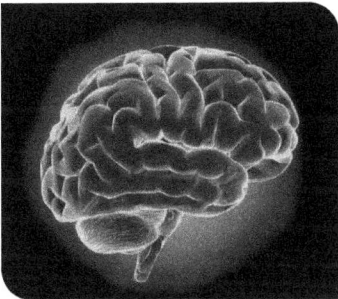

"Whether we like it or not, there is only one thing we can be certain of: things will remain changing in ways we cannot foresee or forecast."

Forbes – July 3,2019

Since I was a little girl, I have been thrilled about the idea of change—rearranging a room, a new paint color, or anything that places me in a different setup. My sister and I exchanged rooms, so we could have that feeling of change when the sunlight entered the room from a different side. I always say that I have a "change chip" in my brain, and it is that "chip" that allows me to adapt easily to any circumstance and look for the bright side of any change.

If you are responsible for change leadership, you have probably wanted to have people with that mentality on your team. However, this attitude is not typical, and to deal with the people you lead, you need to understand how the brain thinks when faced with change to better facilitate change leadership in an organization.

The first thing to understand is that the human brain has been evolving for millions of years to survive in constantly changing circumstances, and, of course, this evolution has been studied for years.

NEUROSCIENCE AND CHANGE

Science gives us the tools to understand causes and tools to use in many business ramifications such as marketing and change management, allowing us to better ourselves as managers.

Neuroscience is now a different world from how it used to be, and now it plays a vital role in change management. In past decades, significant discoveries have transformed how we think about the brain. Every person has a unique brain architecture resulting from the neurological wiring and their experiences, cultural beliefs, and environment.

In his book, "Thinking, Fast and Slow," Daniel

Kahneman (2002 Nobel Laureate in economic science), explains the dual system that our brain uses to process information. His analysis of rationality and reason and understanding how we think and choose allows us to understand why people react to change. These two systems co-exist in the human brain and together help us navigate life.

System 1 is fast and subconscious, and it cannot be turned off. It is also influenced by the context of individuals. It makes intuitive snap judgments based on emotion, memory, and hard-wired rules of thumb. System 1 helps us perform most of the cognitive tasks that everyday life requires. It operates automatically and quickly, with little or no effort and no sense of voluntary control.

System 2 checks the facts and does the math. It allocates attention to the effortful mental activities that demand it, including complex computations. System 2 explores the who, when, and why that surround the decision. System 2 also tends to take shortcuts at the command of System 1. However, System 2 can program System 1 to mobilize attention when a particular pattern is detected.

Some of the fallacies identified by Kahneman are:

- Whatever is easier for System 2 is more likely to be believed. If false concepts are repetitive, our brain accepts it despite knowing it is untrue since the concept becomes familiar and easy to process.
- System 1 jumps to conclusions—we are more open to looking for evidence that supports our beliefs rather than what does not.
- System 1 is prone to consider a recent experience to make decisions and stereotypes to help us decide.

Kahneman shows us that we are at constant risk of repeating the same cognitive errors and biases, and we are easily manipulated and divided by irrational beliefs and fears. Our brain wants to take the path of least resistance. On the other hand, although the division of labor between System 1 and System 2 is highly efficient as it minimizes effort and optimizes performance, it causes conflict in our lives when System 2 tries to overcome the impulses of System 1.

NEUROMARKETING AND THE THREE BRAINS

The natural reaction of our brain to choose things that are easy to understand is what is known as Cognitive Ease and is what companies use in marketing as part of their consumer research (Consumer Neuroscience). Most of the big brands are currently doing neuromarketing to study how consumer minds engage and how they can create stronger connections with their audiences. With this knowledge, brands are now built through emotion to ensure long term memory.

The concept of reptilian brain has gain popularity in the last few years, and it has been used in publications and conference speeches by various experts. Its creator was the American physician and neuroscientist Paul MacLean, M.D., who published the article "The Brain's Generation Gap." He divided the human brain into three main parts differentiated in terms of age and function and called this structure the "triune brain."

1. **The reptilian brain, or primal brain (reptilian complex),** is the oldest of the three and is responsible for the survival response and other primal activities. It controls the body's vital functions such as heart rate, breathing, body temperature, and balance. It is reliable but tends to be rigid and compulsive.

2. **The paleomammalian, or emotional brain (limbic system),** emerged in the first mammals. It is involved with learning, memory, and emotion. The main structures of the Limbic brain are the hippocampus, the amygdala, and the hypothalamus.

3. **The neomammalian, or rational brain (neocortex),** is required for conscious thought and self-awareness. The neocortex is flexible and contains learning abilities. It is also what has enabled human cultures to develop.

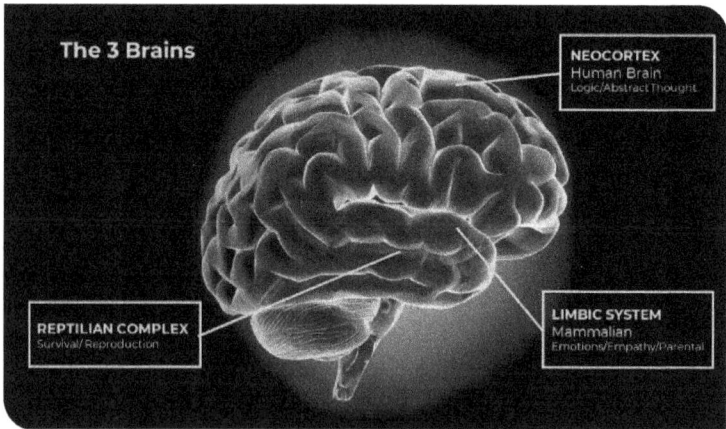

The 3 Brains

NEOCORTEX
Human Brain
Logic/Abstract Thought

REPTILIAN COMPLEX
Survival/Reproduction

LIMBIC SYSTEM
Mammalian
Emotions/Empathy/Parental

The function of the reptilian brain, which drives our instinct and behaviors, retains a good deal of executive control over our actions, while only a small region of the cortex is capable of awareness and articulating its strategies. Each level of the triune brain often battles for dominance simultaneously and conflicts with each other without our conscious awareness.

Neuromarketing, as a concept that applies neuroscience to marketing, is getting attention from companies that want to understand the science behind how people make decisions. This requires them to understand the reptilian part of the brain.

To influence the reptilian part of the brain, company leaders must:

- **Be visual and make it personal:** Use images, as the reptilian brain responds strongly to the visual sense. For example, use posters with no more than eight words, give the benefits, and how it can solve the target audience's problems.
- **Create contrast:** The contrast should show the current situation as unsafe and the new situation as safe—this way, the old brain can make quick, risk-free decisions.
- **Use beginning and ends:** The reptilian brain has a short attention span and can easily forget what is in between. Place the most important message at the beginning.

- **Appeal to the emotions:** The reptilian brain is triggered by emotions (anger, sadness, anxiety, happiness). Many studies demonstrated the impact emotions have on decision-making. Color and fonts play an important role here.

TRANSFORMATION – EMPLOYEE BUY-IN

Understanding how our brain makes decisions and reacts to change, and knowing the techniques used by neuromarketing, we can create a strategy that minimizes the number of frustrated employees who resist change and support our teams as they make decisions that require change.

Decisions can change depending on how they are presented and will be influenced by what is already invested in it. To build a strategic plan, we must take into consideration the following:

1. What is the current situation? The culture, the structure, the comfort, and the habits. What are the strengths and weaknesses?

2. How unhappy is everyone with the current situation? How can we use that as a driver for change?

3. How excited or anxious is the team about the presented change?

As we saw with both theories of the brain, it is human nature (System 1 and the Reptilian Brain) to feel uncomfortable with change; however, we can make it easier by following these steps:

1. Effective communication

The communication should explain the change, include all the details, and should answer the most likely questions that employees will have—the why, what, how, when, and where. **Why** is it happening? Be transparent and make sure that the objectives are clear. **What** are the benefits for the company and for employees, so their System 1 does not jump to conclusions? Show contrast—mark the current situatio as "unsafe" for the future of the company and therefore their future, and the proposed change as the safest approach. This way, the reptilian brain will accept it. **How** the change is going to be implemented, what training they are going to receive, how it will affect their daily functions and the way it will interface with other elements of the process? **When** it is going to happen? Give them the timeline and if it changes, communicate the reasons. **Where** the change is going to happen—is it a companywide change, will it affect only certain departments, what process it will affect, and what personnel will be affected?

2. Break the project into phases:

A plan presented in phases and small steps is less frightening. Avoiding the reptilian brain reaction to unsafe situations will allow you to have repetitive processes and goals that will satisfy System 1 of the brain.

3. Involve people at all levels:

This will appeal to the emotion and the sense of belonging. It will also give you a holistic perspective of the structure and the processes. This selected group of people will act as change ambassadors in their levels. The reptilian brain will have an emotional connection and sense of belonging. The System 1 brain will find it easier to deal with.

SOCIETAL CHANGE, CHANGING PARADIGMS

Our goal is to have a societal change or culture change, and that is why having the company purpose is key. Today, more people of different generations are more connected and perform better when they have a purpose and believe in the purpose of the company and the impact it makes on the world and the environment. On the other hand, loyalty to a company is no longer a rule, and the old ways of employees being disconnected from company decisions are not applicable anymore. We can see this in social media, for good and for bad.

When we change paradigms, we are changing how we think about something. The increase of social media channels such as LinkedIn, allows employees to pressure companies to change their decisions or start acting on hot topics. This new environment is changing the cultural paradigm, and employees want better leaders that listen and accept ideas without judgment based on their own interests.

The recent global lockdown has changed not only our way to work and interact, but it has also changed the way we see the world and our habits. Our beliefs and ideas shift to a different priority list that perhaps was the correct one, to begin with. We are in the middle of disruption, and we do not have the experience or knowledge to guide us. Our pre-existing process and roadmaps are not applicable anymore, and we need to see this paradigm shift as an opportunity where collaboration and networking will help us to have a continuity plan and work across companies and countries to achieve a common goal.

> *"The current events gave us the awareness we need to be willing to act, end the silos, and engage in collaborative leadership to be catalysts for change."*
>
> *Adriana Rosa-Anzule*

TOOL

We know that the human being is predisposed to take the easy way; otherwise, it can create anxiety. Every day we must make hard decisions, and even the simplest tasks, like choosing what to eat or what to wear, have taught us that how we react to any circumstance is up to us. The rise of social media has also created awareness and channels our emotions. **Mindfulness meditation** gained popularity as a tool to help us to reduce stress responses and improve or increase organizational agility and adaptability to change. Companies are seeing positive returns both on an individual level and on an organizational level with the use of this tool. Mindfulness practice impacts brain Systems 1 and 2 and means being present or aware of the current moment, being non-judgmental. Mindfulness is described as a state of mind where System 2 is available, and System 1 is not dominating.

I practice scripture meditation to have a different perspective of the situation, transform my thoughts, align my decisions with my values, and reshape my worldview.

Chapter 2

THE REACTIVE APPROACH

*Look deep inside the ocean of processes to identify
what is not applicable anymore.*

It is human nature to react. It is survival-oriented and, on some level, a defense mechanism. We would rather wait until something happens before we change and, in many cases, we transfer these unconscious decisions to our business.

Let me be clear, I know we all understand that we need to be proactive and respond to situations to the best of our abilities. In the same way, in our business, we have contingency plans and preventative programs. However, I also know that sometimes those plans and programs are done as a necessary task either because it is a regulatory requirement or because it is on the list to have, "just in case."

With all the responsibilities we have and all the processes in the different areas, the preventative programs are low on our priority list. As a result, we end up with a reactive approach. How can we change this? The answer that I receive most of the time is "let's optimize our processes." Optimizing or improving processes many times results in adding more complexity and, in some cases, adds processes on paper that are not actually followed.

For many years, companies have improved their processes on a continuous basis to reduce costs, increase revenue, increase customer satisfaction, and, most importantly, to rise above their competition. It was about competitive advantage. Today's organizations are facing a changing environment that requires more flexibility than ever before. Markets are constantly changing, and companies need to have the ability to react almost immediately to customer demands. Improving the processes is no longer a competitive advantage—it is a survival tool to help build an effective structure that supports the company's capabilities.

The question here is how can we master that survival tool? My answer: we need to SIMPLIFY. It sounds easy but is not, and we need to be brave. We need to break the existing paradigms and prove that simplicity can be a powerful weapon for survival.

We live in a society that demands more and more and is not pleased until things are in a high level of complexity that provides a sense of accomplishment. Society taught us that if things are simple, something is not right or is not worth it; that simple things are for lazy people, for losers. We grew up with that mentality; therefore, we need to show that we are capable of solving big and complex problems to feel powerful and proud of our job.

This is how we ended up in a maze of complex situations, with processes that do not apply in the current volatile world or processes that are obsolete, because, in only one year, the industry advanced five years, if not more. We need to accept reality; we need to understand that our current processes are not a true reflection of what we need, but the result of prior experience mixed with our inability to simplify and say, "No".

The value of simplicity has been underestimated, and I passionately believe that embracing simplicity is the only way to survive in these uncertain times. Being able to use straightforward, simple strategies to adapt to the market, the customer demand, the internal requirements, and the environment--without losing the focus and purpose of the company—is key for a business to maintain its advantage and be able to grow.

"I choose a lazy person to do a hard job. Because a lazy person will find an easy way to do it."

- Bill Gates

Companies cannot wait for things to go back to normal because they are not going to! Instead, they need to start changing, to simplify, and adapt. We need to shape things down in all areas to provide more flexibility and efficiency, and at the same time, simplify the process to make things clear, concrete, easy to understand, adaptable, repeatable, and accessible.

Embracing a simplified version of the process

requires a new mindset. Not only is it necessary to establish a clear strategy and detailed design principles, but we also need to look for ways to make everyone's life easier and ensure that those processes will add value to the customer by expediting the cycle or giving them more flexibility.

We need to think that our customers are on the same road—they are confronting the same challenging changes that we are, and they also need to respond to the market fluctuations. If we start thinking about the customer's needs beyond their demands and forecasts, we can secure our advantage. However, to do this, we need to first look at how complex the structure of the company is and perform a deep evaluation. We need to scrutinize and find the processes that are obsolete or will not be adaptable enough to the new rapid environment. We need to identify what is not applicable anymore and make sure that what we have is simple enough to give us the flexibility to respond to the customer's needs.

THE 5 WS

A good methodology to follow while we gather the information to understand the cause of the complexity of our processes is the 5 Ws. Answering these questions can help us to discover how much we can simplify them.

What? What is happening? What is our end goal? What processes are constraining our speed to respond and adapt to change? Past processes were designed to perform specific activities and changes. They did not happen frequently. Therefore, companies and, more specifically, employees did not acquire good skills that allowed them to master those processes.

Now, in the volatile environment that we live in today, companies add and combine activities to accomplish a multitude of tasks simultaneously, changing the focus. However, many times the organizational structure and the design of the processes do not allow it. What once had a short life can be obsolete in days.

Why? Why is the process needed? Can we eliminate it? Can it be combined? If the objective is clear, why is it so difficult to develop procedures that give us the required flexibility to add value to our customers while making our lives easier? The answer can be found in our own human nature. We are incapable of immediately saying no because since we were little, we have been taught that saying yes makes you good and saying no makes you the bad one or the loser. Therefore, our brain is programmed to look for the pleasure of being the good one. The why is the most important: Why do we do it?

Who? This is a difficult question, and perhaps many of us immediately answer "those who perform the task," or others think "those who write or design the processes." However, processes are not written and documented for the person who is already doing it. They are written for people who are coming in new or for people who do not know the specific details. Do we have all the processes we need so that anyone can understand how the business runs?

When? This, in my opinion, can give more complexity to the process and at the same time, restrain us. Some processes are exceptions to the rule or are required on an exceedingly rare occasion. Why make them general and applicable for our day-to-day operations? In these cases, I recommend creating an amendment or an appendix section that explains the situations where the processes are applicable. To simplify, we need to categorize and eliminate generalizations that create more complexity.

Where? Once again, we need to avoid generalizations. If it only applies to a specific area or a specific site, do not generalize it. We need to reprogram our brain and understand that less is not bad; instead, less can give us the agility to adapt.

THE ROUTE TO SIMPLIFICATION

Simplification is an art. It is the ability to transform existing complex situations or processes into something easier to understand with fewer steps, without affecting its effectiveness. I like to explain it in math terms. Remember when we had to reduce a fraction to the lowest terms? It represents the same amount—they are equal terms—however, the lowest term is easier to understand. To use a famous phrase: "Simplicity is not a destination. It is a journey." Simplicity needs to support growth and future regulatory changes, and it needs to be evaluated constantly. We need to put simplicity as the center of our business model in order to be able to compete with the chaos of societal disruptions.

Back in 2012, Andrew Haldane, Chief Economist at the Bank of England, gave the best explanation of the importance of simplicity. He was the executive director at that time. Mr. Haldane explained why border collies could catch a frisbee better than many humans, including ones with physics PhDs. He explained that although it is a common game, catching a frisbee requires you to process, in real-time, a complicated set of physical and atmospheric factors: wind, gravity, the frisbee's rotation, and flight path. With this statement, he explained that you do not need to understand the complex science behind it to be able to play. Furthermore, if you tried to think it through, your brain would be overwhelmed, and you would not be able to catch the frisbee. Border Collies do not understand the science behind it; they keep it simple and catch it. Mr. Haldane stated that in complex decision-making problems, simple rules do as well as complex solutions.

For years, we are living in a world that is constantly changing, and instability is increasing. Neither of these is new. Although we are hearing more and more these days, the word VUCA (Volatile, Uncertain, Complex, and Ambiguous) has been used in military education since 1987.

In the last fifteen years, it became more difficult to predict the market and use historical data to anticipate and create good strategies. Having a clear picture of the situations is almost impossible, not because of a lack of effort, but because of uncertainty and the multiple options available. Decisions are now more of a reaction than the result of studies and planning.

Having a robust, and at the same time flexible, framework is particularly important. As I mentioned before, we need to rewire our brain and understand that it is possible to have a robust system that is, at the same time, flexible and simple. We need some time right now to understand this concept, so let me repeat it. It is possible to have a simple, agile, and flexible, robust system!

How? Here is where the strategy is important. We need to have the right group of people with the right set of skills and mindset. We need to change the culture of the business and eliminate the idea that complexity is a synonym of sophistication, and simplicity is a sign of weakness.

With all the advances in technology and artificial intelligence (AI), many are worried about the impact on human jobs. Although many experts say that several professions will be automated and completely replaced by AI in coming years, the soft skills that only humans can provide are still necessary. Humans will be redirected, jobs will be more efficient, and they need to be simpler.

MAS METHODOLOGY

After doing the exercise of the 5 Ws and gaining a better picture of the current stage, we can start the simplification process using the simple MAS methodology that has three phases:

Phase 1: Micro-Analysis

- Look for what changes are needed in order to

be more flexible—flexible to customer demands, flexible to adapt to constant changes, and flexible for employees. Make sure the directions are clear, and you have a streamlined communication process, both internal and external.

- It is important to look beyond the process. Look at overly layered communications, the file systems (both physical paper and shared hard drives), and the number of people in emails and meetings. A good rule for reducing the number of people on emails is visualization. Would you invite all the people if the information was distributed at a meeting? If the answer is no, then remove them.

- Look for what is obsolete or does not apply anymore. Here it is important to get out of the box and really think. Our brain is going to play it safe and tell us this is how we always do it, and it works. Consider that you need to be brave and ready to change the status quo—you will be able to achieve what you need to in a different way.

- Look for processes and structures that do not give you any value and are simply "good to have it." I guarantee you that later, those "good to have" items can tie your hands. Remember, our end goal is agility and flexibility. You can have multiple customers, requirements, processes, and services and still implement simplicity. The key is to find the point where simplicity and efficacy can work together.

- Look deeper, look for those processes that are not written, but everyone follows because they are part of the DNA of the company. I like to illustrate this important step with our daily lives. If you are a person that likes to write lists and document all the tasks that you must do the next day, I am quite sure that you will not list "brush my teeth." Why? Because it is something that is automated in your brain. You do not need to think about it. You just do it. Those are the processes that you need to look for and evaluate if they are still necessary or not applicable anymore.

- Evaluate the operational model and strategy. Both need to have the flexibility to adapt to the constant changes and disruptions without compromising integrity and quality.

Phase 2: Adapt

- This is the transformative phase, where you implement the changes you identified in Phase 1.

- Eliminate unnecessary tasks, steps, and interactions, and have a defined and clear desired outcome.

- In this phase, you can standardize and add new technology and artificial intelligence that simplify the processes.

- Remove the layers of organizational complexity and intricate approval systems that prevent growth, reduce agility, and the capacity to respond to the customer.

- Ensure that all activities are productive. A key point here is to eliminate unnecessary meetings and make sure that people have an agenda before the meeting That they have a clear idea of why they are in the meeting, what information they need to bring, and what follow up items they are responsible for. This will eliminate unnecessary subsequent meetings.

- Design the process to embrace change. The strategy and operational models must be flexible enough to adapt to different circumstances, but at the same time, they need to be robust enough to support growth. The structure of your strategy must be simple to understand and execute; it should provide an easy way to plan and create goals. Defining the correct operating model is imperative in order to obtain a simple and agile process that ensures clarity, efficiency, and alignment with the company vision.

- The most important task is to adapt to a new culture where simplicity is valued. Employees need to understand that adopting simplicity is an act of courage and intelligence, that it requires new behavior, a rewired brain where we consciously look for ways to simplify and eliminate the complexity of the day-to-day tasks and decisions.

Phase 3: Sustain

- In this phase, it is important to reinforce the implementations and changes.
- Evaluate, measure, and data analysis must be a daily task. However, the task does not end there. We need to put data into action and have a holistic analysis. The times of isolated data by area or department has ended. We need to analyze how the data of one area affects another one and understand not only the trends and capabilities but the available responses. Data is now a company asset, and the platform should not be limited to one department or group.

- Establish continuous improvement programs that look for the optimization of the processes and guarantee simplicity every day, with every decision.
- Ensure that all processes and activities are aligned with the strategy and the purpose and value of the company.
- Evaluate the implementation of new technology to ensure that it adds value, not complexity. Understand that the lines between IT and the other departments will disappear in the future as data literacy increases and technology is simplified.
- Ensure that even in the middle of disruption, the business has a clear vision to drive simplicity.

"Life is really simple, but we insist on making it complicated."

- Confucius

Once we have simplified our processes and structures, we can prepare our survival tool. I am convinced that the reactive approach cannot be part of our business anymore; therefore, we need to start our proactive approach. In a world of uncertainty and constant change, optimizing and simplifying our process is not enough. We need to repeat the three phases again and **RSVP** to take our business to a **R**idiculously **S**imple **V**ersion **P**rocess. This will be the only way to survive.

I believe that a new group of business leaders will rise— leaders that will be willing to kill their ego and simplify their processes to a ridiculously simple version. Leaders who believe that simplicity is the weapon of the future. Professionals with a new mindset to lead using the tools that a good process can give.

TOOL

The following tools can be used in the different phases of the MAS methodology:

Micro-Analysis Phase:

The SWOT Analysis tool will help to find the areas that need help and how to minimize risk. This tool will show the non-value-added tasks as well.

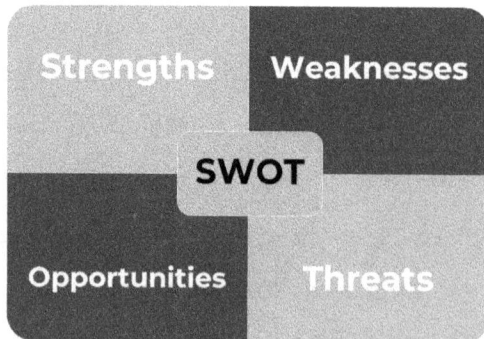

Adapt Phase

This model is a simple approach to evaluate the strategy or road map to achieve goals. It looks at the four factors that allow transforming inputs into outputs, giving you a holistic view of the components of the organization.

NADLER – TUSHMAN CONGRUENCE FRAMEWORK

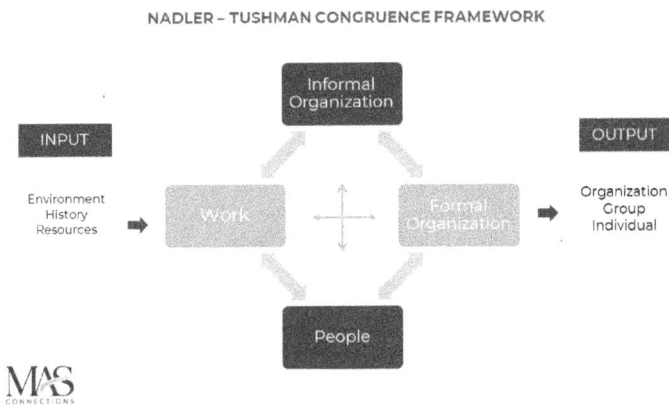

Sustain Phase:

To evaluate the strategy:

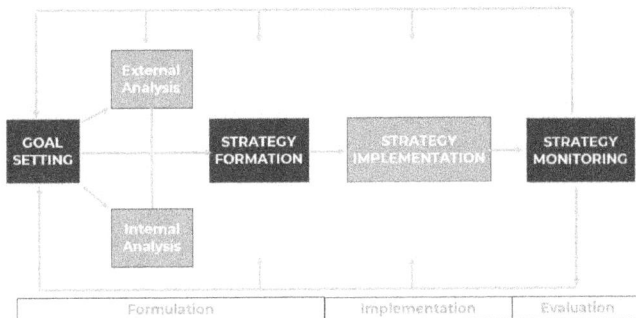

Chapter 3

THE RIPPLE EFFECT

Evaluating the impact of a change

Every change or implementation requires a phase of planning where the impact is evaluated along with the risks; however, we cannot eliminate from the equations the ripple effect. The ripple effect are those situations in which a series of events happen as a result of a change or a particular event, usually unintentionally. This effect can be positive or negative and it can occur in the process or in the people. The ripple effect can also extend outside the business. This happens when an internal change led to a cultural change or a customer behavior change. Could you imagine if your company is the driver of a massive shift in society?

I do not want to talk about the risk analysis and the planning of a change or implementation as I do not believe that is the real issue. In my experience, I have noticed that companies are doing a fair job, looking at how the areas of the business interrelate and how the process and tasks affect the different areas. The effects on people, the training, and the opportunities are also covered. In addition, you can find plenty of information about this topic with the details on how to perform the risk analysis, and the methodologies and templates to cover the planning phase.

I want to talk about what happens beyond the obvious; about what happens deep inside the ocean of process and personnel, strategies and data, innovation, and artificial intelligence. Deep, where we believe nothing happens.

THE OCEAN

I invite you to close your eyes and think about the ocean. Some people like the ocean when it is calm and they can enjoy the serenity and peace and have some swimming time. On the other hand, others like the ocean when the waves are high, and they can surf. I always think that a business is like the ocean, and if we learned more about the ocean, we could understand more about how to manage our businesses.

Scientists explain that the ocean surface is the critical junction for energy exchange between the atmosphere and the deep ocean. In the same way, a business is the exchange between the customers, the market (atmosphere), and the deep ocean (the company structure and pillars).

Changes in the surface will cause changes in the amount of heat and momentum being exchanged between the surface and the deep sea. In the same way a change in the market will cause changes in the way we need to operate and respond to the customer, and at the same time will affect the energy of our company.

For many years, we were in a calm ocean where small waves come in regular intervals, rising, moving forward, losing their strength, and coming back. Therefore, in our businesses we established a process for a day at the beach, where we can swim and play. We also have contingency processes, for times when the friction between the surface water and the wind creates waves. In those instants, we grab our surf boards and enjoy the moment.

The ocean currents driven by winds, water density, and tides can teach us how all the external factors affect our businesses. Regulations, changes in the environment, the market, and even problems in other countries can have a direct impact on our business.

At the same time, differences in water density, resulting from the variability of water temperature and salinity, also cause ocean currents. Here we can think on the company culture (temperature) and the skill set or training (salinity).

DEEP WATERS

Deep waters are "formed" where the air temperatures are cold and where the salinity of the surface waters are relatively high. The combinations of salinity and cold temperatures make the water denser and cause it to sink to the bottom. One important factor of the deep ocean is the lack of light; light is almost absent.

In our business, we all know that life in the deep waters is unexplored and the absence of light, or knowledge of those processes, make them irrelevant during any analysis. I include in these deep waters all those processes that are intrinsic to the company, those process that were established at the beginning stages of the company, and happen almost automatically in the backend, to the point that they are forgotten. Nevertheless, those deep-water processes and tasks are crucial to our business, as they provide support, structure, and are part of the culture of the business. Only by looking at what is in the deep ocean of our business can we guarantee that any change or implementation will have a good ripple effect and can be sustained.

Unfortunately, you cannot see the ripple effect of a rock when is dropped into the water if you are inside the water. You need to be on shore to have good visibility of how the rock will push water out of its way as it enters, causing ripples to move away from its point of entry in a circle. Therefore, I invite you to get out of the water and analyze the ripple effects of the plans and changes of your company.

"Even in the middle of a hurricane, the bottom of the sea is calm. As the storm rages and the winds howl, the deep waters sway in gentle rhythm, a light movement of fish and plant life. Below there is no storm."

- Wayne Muller

STREAMLINING BUSINESS PROCESSES

Going back to the ocean example, identify the processes that are not efficient, obsolete, or do not apply anymore. It can be like scuba diving, when you enter the underwater world you start seeing more and more interesting things. The success of process improvement or streamlining is seen when you look for those that are not obvious, those that are underwater. Once you identify them, you can start the prioritization process, always keeping in mind the possible connections. Doing this is necessary to understand the process, the documentation, as well as the personnel roles, and their interaction with the process, including the frequency.

Steps to Evaluate a Process

Process review is not only good practice but is

necessary to keep the agility in your business. Any unnecessary tasks are just adding weight and delaying the entire cycle in the respective area. Evaluating the process periodically will also help to identify new strengths and weakness due to the constantly changing environment. Following the next steps for each process helps to streamline and simplify them.

- Review the scope and purpose of the process.
- Review the responsible parties and verify that all involved are listed, and that none are missing.
- Analyze the steps and tasks. Are those aligned with the goal and scope?
- Identify tasks that are not applicable anymore or are obsolete.
- Identify tasks that can be simplified or combined.
- Identify tasks that do not add value to the company or the department.
- Identify tasks that can be automated.
- Evaluate the deliveries and any additional support documentation.
- It is recommended to interview the personnel; sometimes the actual process differs from the documented process.

Process Mapping

Most of the time it is easier to understand what is happening with a process where we can have a visual representation of the steps, cycle time, and the resources involved. Being able to see the relationship between the input and the tasks, why they are performed, who performed in what frequency, what documentation is required, and then, what the output and logistics are.

Business process mapping (BPM) can provide the necessary understanding to be able to standardize, improve the process results, and simplify. Business process mapping can also be used for training; it is easier for the human brain to register visual examples. In the planning phase of an implementation, where the impact is evaluated, gives more detailed information, reducing the risk of mistakes or inaccuracies. It will also serve as a reference point or proof of compliance in regulatory audits.

Some of the benefits of mapping a business process are:

- **Clarity:** Everyone will see the process as it really is. It increases consistency and reduces the risk of errors. It also helps in problem solving and decision making.

- **Cross functional understanding:** It gives visibility

of the impact that each process has in the different areas. It can be used to analyze risk as well as for the standardization.

- **Accountability:** It is easy to see the responsible parties and the phase of intervention.
- **Change:** Process mapping is used as a baseline and easily shows the before and after when a change occurred.
- **Compliance:** Process mapping can demonstrate compliance with regulatory requirements such as FDA and ISO, as well as company and customer Standard Operating Procedures (SOPs).
- **Continuous improvement:** Process mapping facilitates improvement in the process as it identifies waste, risk, bottlenecks, delays, and capacity constraints. In the same way, it is easier to see where the process can be streamlined.

To perform a good process mapping it is necessary to understand the scope, what is included and what is not. It is important to keep it simple, without excluding a step. It is also important to get thorough information from the stakeholders, people that perform the task, as well as the supervisors and managers. This is the only way to obtain the process map as it is and not as it should be. The most common types of business process maps are the Value Stream Map, and the Swimlane or Cross-functional Map that separates out the sub-process responsibilities in the process.

In Business Process Mapping the symbols are standardized. These symbols come from the Unified Modeling Language (UML), which is an international standard for drawing process maps. In the table below you can find the most common ones.

Start		Decision	
Process Step		Date	
Document		Multiple Documents	
Page Connector		Flow or Connector	
Artifact		Database	
Manual		Delay	

EVALUATING THE IMPACT

When evaluating the impact of a change, every manager or team has his point of view, based on his personal experience, the environment they are in, the culture of the company, and his vision of the change. The evaluation is more subjective than objective, even though they will say that it is not. Once again, it is in our nature, it is the way our brain processes the information. Change management has changed during the years. Before, the impact of a change was focused on the equipment, buildings, and other physical assets. Later, the focus changed to the culture, the leadership, and the personnel training. Although these factors are important, if they are evaluated alone or in an isolated environment, it will give us the wrong data.

To have a complete and more accurate analysis, we must evaluate two main group of factors:

Resources or Hard Factors

These factors are quantifiable, and their impact is easier to be measure. When analyzing the impact of resources, it is important to look at the weaknesses and the strengths. Under resources we have:

- Financial resources: The cost of the change or implementation and the benefits the company will gain are evaluated. The benefit is based on the purpose of the change. The duration of the change or implementation directly affects these resources, therefore the risk analysis for delays should be included. Here the budget and sources of income must be clear.

- Human resources: A comprehensive list of the available personnel for every stage of the change or implementation is needed as well as a list of the direct personnel affected with the change. It is important to select leaders who generate trust. This way, the communication will be easier, and the motivation will increase. Another point to take into consideration is the skill set of the personnel. This should be taken into consideration as this directly affects the duration of the change. (More training might be required.)

- Physical resources: This includes facilities, locations, equipment, and software. To evaluate the physical resources, you need to play a chess game. You need to know how to move your pieces, and more importantly, which one you move first. The first location is imperative for the success of the entire plan. A successful one can motivate others and give the executives some peace of mind.

Soft Factors

These factors are culture, leadership, motivation, and adaptability. These factors are qualitative, and although they are not measured by a number, it can be analyzed by how they add value to the company (positive, negative, or minimal effect). The culture of a company needs to be analyzed in two phases—the culture of the company as a whole and the culture of each location. Since the culture is developed with time and is the result of the beliefs, behaviors, past practices, and assumptions that have contributed to its success, it will never be the same between two facilities or locations.

To have a good evaluation of the impact, it is important to look at both the numbers of the hard factors as well as the influences and qualities of the soft factors. As many studies in change management show, the most common reasons for a change failure are the ability to change the mindset of the personnel to embrace change, and underestimating the complexity of the project, which affects the duration and cost of the project.

As I mentioned earlier, you can find great and valuable information about change management. However, each company and each project are different, and not all rules apply in the same way. What it is important is to evaluate the relevant aspects of the project in your location and defining phases and tasks. Identifying potential threats and developing scenarios that show what could happen is also a good practice.

"Complexity is the enemy of execution."

- Tony Robbins

Measuring the Impact

We should measure the impact of any change at different phases of the project, emphasizing the planning phase. The first step should be talking to the personnel that is going to be directly affected (stakeholders). Understand and analyze their concerns, but also their expectations. It is important to create trust and select the right team for this; it should be people that understand the processes and the purpose of the change--people with the ability to deliver confidence while they go underwater, deep into the real perceptions of the people. If we understand their fears and we can address them in the earlier phases, we can avoid the resistance that jeopardize any change.

How the information is going to be collected and analyzed is another important factor. It cannot be limited to surveys. It needs to have a combination of methods depending on the type of change, the area, and the amount of personnel affected. It is important to limit the scope when evaluating to really understand the cultural impact as well.

OUT OF THE WATER

We looked deep in the ocean, and now is time to get out of the water to see the ripple effect. How has the change impacted the company? What is the culture of the company? Did it have a good effect on the customers? Did the change achieve the objectives? Did the project have delays? Were issues encountered? What was the root cause for those problems? How do the employees feel now? Did you identify new aspects that can be improved?

Once we have the answers to these questions, we can see the impact of the change and, moreover, the ripple effect. The change, if successful, promotes a new way of thinking, a new behavior, not only among the people but the entire structure (customers, suppliers, etc.) that reinforce the company purpose and vision, making the company stronger. If the changes are around sustainability, the ripple effect is greater. The entire world is looking at the company's standards, and changes in those areas directly affect the reputation of the brand. Companies and brands are evaluated for their corporate social responsibility and environmental response, and how it impacts the community and their economic conditions.

During the pandemic, we saw another ripple effect on a more global scale, the supply chain. Almost every business has been affected by the effects of the shutdowns and the border closings. The supply chain risks were evaluated before, at a completely different scale, without even considering the nature of today's problems. At the same time, this pandemic shows us the weaknesses and challenges of our supply change management programs.

It is important that companies look deep into their supply chain management to increase visibility and control, reduce cycle times, and to have different options that allow for the agility and flexibility required to react to any type of disruption in the new global structure. It is not only the changes in the demand that forces companies to quickly act to avoid the financial capacity impact, we also need to consider the potential disruptions.

Simplicity in the supply chain can be a key differentiator and it can reduce the risk and increase the flexibility. It will also give the essential agility to recover from a disruption. Perhaps the new project in our companies can be to evaluate the supply change model to identify the weakness and the opportunities and implement changes that guarantee a company's performance and growth.

Having standardized and reliable information available on a timely basis, across the entire organization, will allow us to adapt to the changes in demand faster and have better strategies to create a unique and sustainable competitive position. The supply chain models that were created to lower the costs by having single suppliers are not applicable anymore. Companies now need to invest in flexible ecosystems of suppliers that can handle sudden changes in demand and also in platforms and tools that increase information sharing. This should be done not only internally, but with the suppliers and the customers, with real time visibility that allows the analysis of the data to have projections and different capacity scenarios.

TOOLS ───────────────

- To evaluate how an individual adapts to a change and moves from his Current Stage to the Future Stage, you can use the Prosci ADKAR® model that describes the 5 areas for successful change.

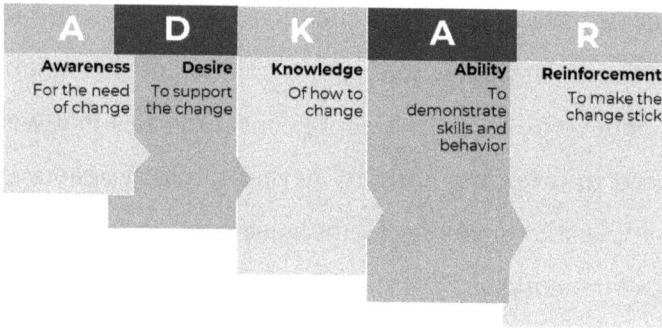

A	D	K	A	R
Awareness	Desire	Knowledge	Ability	Reinforcement
For the need of change	To support the change	Of how to change	To demonstrate skills and behavior	To make the change stick

- Another tool to use is Dr. Kotter 8 steps process for leading change:

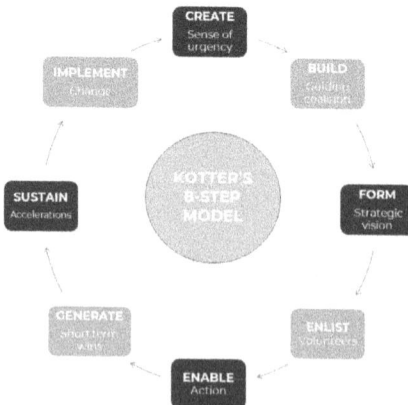

Chapter 4

YESTERDAY'S DECISION-MAKING FRAMEWORK

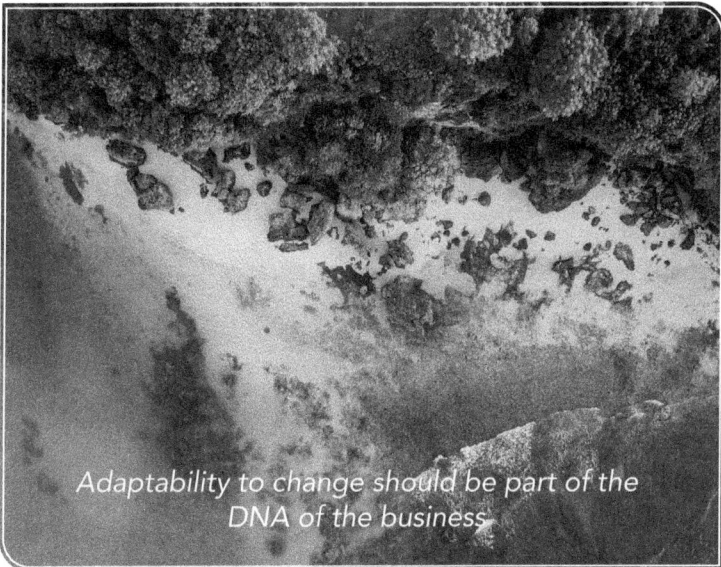

Adaptability to change should be part of the DNA of the business

NOT APPLICABLE ANYMORE

It is easy to see that the decision-making process has changed drastically. In today's world, it is imperative to make decisions in a short period of time. Risk management evolved thanks to the increased knowledge of human behavior and the amount of data that technology put into our hands. These factors improved not only the speed but also the quality and the ability to identify challenges, threats, and opportunities.

If we look at the past, initiatives used to take around five years to plan, be implemented, and then used. Company strategies included long and short-term goals, and the decision-making process was managed by a small group of high-level executives behind closed doors and without the involvement of other managers or employees. Past experience was commonly used as a factor for decision making, and strategies were less complex and systematic.

Decision making was clearly classified into three categories based on the level at which they occur:

1. Strategic decisions that set the course of an organization.
2. Tactical decisions that affected how things would get done.
3. Operational decisions that employees made each day to run the organization.

Companies are organized around the "Scientific Method" or the "Command of Control" models of

1910 with some changes and improvements. Concepts like policies and procedures, management layers, and production lines are concepts that were successful for many years due to long-term stable conditions. The market and fixed forecasts allowed the investment of single purpose equipment with highly trained staff and elaborate plans to minimize risk.

These conditions are not applicable anymore. Technology increased the ability to obtaining information that changed the market (cost and value) and created fluid forecasts. Current circumstances (before the pandemic) do not allow the specific allocation of resources, increasing the risk, and reducing the specialty of both equipment and employees. Management layers can be a disadvantage as they impact the ability of decision making. Agility and customer experience are now the main advantages of a company.

If we add the challenges of the pandemic we are facing today, almost nothing of what we have established as a business model and decision-making process will be applicable anymore. The environment changed, the priorities changed, the customer requirements changed— our world changed.

A HOLISTIC VIEW OF A COMPANY BUSINESS STRUCTURE

We need a holistic view of the business structure, process, and strategy, and now it is more imperative than ever as we are facing global disruptive situations. We must look from the outside, where we can have a clear picture of the entire organization, as a whole, interconnected entity. Evaluating each department for their inner strengths and weaknesses, but also regarding how they relate to every other aspect of the company.

Let's start by understanding the basic concepts that sometimes, depending on the complexity of the company, are not easy to differentiate.

Company Structure: The structure is how the company is organized and how the work is done. In other words, is it organized by departments within a location (decentralized), or is it organized by functions despite the location (centralized). The structure outlines how certain activities are directed in order to achieve the goals of an organization. It will also determine how information flows between the different levels within the company. The structure determines if the proper people are in place to adequately execute the strategy.

Company Processes: The processes are how activities are done, how they move from one phase to another, how decisions are made, how information flows, how business units interact, and how resources are allocated. Processes are the driving force of a company and can direct the agility to respond to a disruption or new business.

Company Strategy: The strategy is the roadmap of the company, the set of guiding principles and rules that defines how things will be done to accomplish business goals and to secure a competitive position.

Once we have a clear understanding of the structure, processes, and strategy of the company, we can evaluate what is not applicable anymore and define how it should be addressed. This is an exercise that should not be done alone; it is crucial that we engage the employees and empower them to think about the entire business and the ramifications of their decision-making at the same time they abandon the silos and departmental mentality.

DECISION MAKING IS NOT ONLY A SKILL, IT IS AN ART

One of the more significant decision-making failures in modern business history was when Blockbuster decided not to buy Netflix. Decision-making is a skill that is getting more challenging every day as a result of the conditions of disruption, uncertainty, and risk. Decision making is not only a skill; it is the art of managing these basic elements:

- Establishing a positive decision-making environment
- Generating potential solutions
- Evaluating the solutions
- Deciding
- Checking the decision
- Communicating and implementing

---

*"Good decisions come from experience.
Experience comes from making bad decisions."*

- Mark Twain

We know that rapid and precise decision-making is critical for any business to survive. We have also learned that our brains are wired to protect us from risky and uncertain situations, generating obstacles. To be able to have a good decision-making process, we must reduce the obstacles by identifying them and learning how to manage them.

1. **Indecision:** Indecision is caused by uncertainty, fear, and insecurity and paralyzes us when making decisions. How can we reduce them or cope?

    a. **Uncertainty:** We can reduce uncertainty by gathering information, collaboration, and networking.

b. **Fear:** The most common fears are fear of failure, loss, and rejection. Fear is often subconscious and self-sabotages our good intentions. Overcoming fear is a skill that we all need. First, we need to understand the fear by responding to this question: What exactly am I afraid of? Then we need to think of the worst-case scenario and realize that after this analysis, we can overcome our fears.

c. **Insecurity:** I believe that we do not overcome insecurity, but we can embrace it and use it as a transformative force, as the fuel that gives us the power to deal with any circumstance.

2. **Cognitive Biases:** Part of our brain's wiring triggers these biases and occurs from our need to make sense of a situation before deciding on a course of action. Identifying the biases, we experience the first step to understanding how we make decisions based on a predisposition of our mind instead of evidence. This can help us make better and more informed decisions. The most common biases are:

a. **Confirmation bias:** The tendency to seek out information that supports something you already believe.

b. **In-group bias:** Removes objectivity from any sort of selection or hiring process as we tend to favor those we personally know and want to help.

c. **Self-serving bias:** Results in a tendency to blame outside circumstances for bad situations rather than taking personal responsibility.

d. **Availability bias:** The tendency to use the information we can quickly recall when evaluating a topic or idea, even if wrong.

e. **Fundamental attribution error:** The tendency to attribute someone's particular behaviors to existing, unfounded stereotypes.

f. **Hindsight bias:** Can lead to overconfidence in one's ability to predict future outcomes.

g. **Anchoring bias:** Refers to those who rely too heavily on the first piece of information they receive.

h. **Optimism bias:** We are more likely to estimate a positive outcome if we are in a good mood.

i. **Pessimism bias:** We are more likely to estimate a negative outcome if we are in a bad mood.

j. **The halo effect:** This refers to our overall impression of a person; it influences how we feel and think about their character.

     k. Status quo bias: The preference to keep things in their current state.

3. **Data Strain:** We must know when to make decisions with the information we have on hand and when we need to delay the process to gather more information. Technology allows us to access large amounts of data and have it in real-time, which not only can be overwhelming but also can affect the decision-making process. To be valuable, the data needs to be consolidated and organized for fast, easy retrieval in a coherent manner; we also need to be able to analyze it and understand how to use it.

4. **Lack of Purpose:** If we evaluate the impact the company is having on society, we can open a door of possibilities for change and growth. If the company does not have a clear purpose, core values will not have that impact, and making the right decisions will become more challenging. The stability of having a clear purpose and core values is vital in the volatile environment we have. Having a "why" provides a moral direction to guide the decision-making.

"When your values are clear to you, making decisions becomes easier."

- Roy Disney

DATA-DRIVEN DECISION-MAKING

Data-driven decision-making was a competitive advantage that reduced business costs and increased profit. Now it is a requirement to survive. The old ways of making decisions based on experience or history are not applicable anymore. The world is not the same, and there have been significant changes that make past methods obsolete.

Data is only as valuable as the insights you can get from it. The metrics and KPIs we use will define how effective our data-driven decisions are.

1. **Identify Business Goals and Strategy:** Look at your business objectives, then build a strategy around them.

2. **Find the Proper KPIs and Metrics:** Keep only the most valuable data that will help with your decision-making.

3. **Collect and Analyze**: Identify trends, analyze external factors that have a direct effect on the data, and keep it in mind when making decisions. Make sure the data is accessible—the more people who have access, the greater the possibility of getting insights from the data.

4. **Get Conclusions:** Present the data in a meaningful

way; the data should tell a story. Remember, our brain responds better to visual cues rather than text alone. Use data dashboards, with this information tool you can visually track and display key performance indicators (KPI), metrics to monitor the business, or a specific process.

5. **Measure and Improve**: Never stop measuring and questioning your data-driven decisions, and do not be afraid to change it. Both external factors, as well as internal changes, can make your KPIs and metrics obsolete at any given moment.

Data is now a critical enterprise asset. We must ensure that everyone has access and be ambassadors for a culture that encourages critical thinking based on data, a culture that develops and trains in data proficiency and analytics agility. This can be the path to success in the current fluid environment.

DECISION-MAKING TECHNIQUES

The decision-making process involves various steps, and it is important that we follow a structured method or technique to be effective—some of these techniques we use in our daily lives without even noticing it.

1. **Decision Matrix:** This technique is used when a decision needs to be made between multiple variables. It is similar to the pros and cons list that we use when we need to make a decision in our personal lives. The difference here is that each factor must be placed on a level of importance. To do it, we need to list the alternatives in rows and the factors in columns and then assign them a value in the order of importance. The option that scores the highest is the one to select.

2. **SWOT Diagram:** This technique helps us to have a better picture of the factors that influence the situation by listing the strengths, weaknesses, opportunities, and threats. This exercise should be done in a collaborative environment; this way, we can have a more holistic approach and ensure all variants are taken into consideration.

3. **Pareto Analysis:** Sometimes, we have multiple things to change; however, not all can be done at the same time. How do we choose? The pareto analysis is a principle that states that 20 percent of factors frequently contribute to 80 percent of the organization's growth. Therefore, if we can identify what small changes will make the largest

impact, we will be able to prioritize the decisions that have the highest level of transformation.

4. **Affinity Diagrams:** This is a technique that can help when we have large amounts of data. It is a visual brainstorming tool that allows teams to organize ideas into groups according to their natural relationships. To create an affinity diagram, we just need to record the ideas, then look for related concepts or connections and group them together. Finally, we combine the groups into master groups to synthesize the ideas into a more cohesive whole.

YESTERDAY'S FRAMEWORK

We can see more companies every day that are closing their doors after many years in business. Personally, the one that made me sad was Toys R Us. One of the main reasons these companies are disappearing is the obsolete business models that cannot adapt to the conditions and speed of the new market. Business models have been evolving, as shown below.

1. **1900-1950, Mass Production Business Models:** Ford is a perfect example for this business model, with the creation of mass production lines that

reduced costs and increased productivity. Here (100 years ago) is where technology innovation started to be an advantage for a company, and the concept of standardization gained popularity. As I mentioned at the beginning of the chapter, these concepts of line production and cost reduction are the basis of many of the current manufacturing businesses.

2. **1950-1990, Marketing Business Models:** The economy after World War II motivated people to buy homes, cars, clothes, and products to validate their lifestyles. Production continued to expand more quickly than the growth in demand for goods and services, creating the start of the marketing era. The new marketing concepts changed the mentality of businesses, and they started thinking about the necessities of the customer and having better products and services than the competition.

3. **1990-2010, Internet Business Models:** The impact that the internet had on business during this time was enormous. It created new business models, but also company structures and the popular information-centric companies. The

internet became a force that transformed every aspect not only for the business but for the life of each of the customers. This era was the beginning of the biggest companies we see today—Microsoft, Google, Amazon, Yahoo. These companies, thanks to the internet, did in little time what many other brick and mortar companies were trying for many years. One good example was Yahoo, who in only two years (1997 to 1999) evolved from a simple web browser to the multi-billion-dollar media company that we know today. Another big advantage for business in this era was the possibility of creating scalable business structures for a global market. The internet changed the economy models as well; with access to information, the previous models of economic growth were not applicable anymore.

4. **2010-2020, Customer-Centric Business Models:** The internet helped the businesses but also provided information to the customer, and as we know, information is power. Businesses changed from being product-centric to customer-centric. The customer started asking for what they

wanted and challenged the companies through the use of social media. Companies started to study the necessities and behavior of the customer. Previously, businesses started taking advantage of neuroscience knowledge and started using neuromarketing, segmentation, and many other tools that allowed them to maximize the interaction with the ideal buyer persona.

5. **Business models after 2020?** I believe that it is safe to say that the new business models will be data-driven without changing the focus on the customer. The customer will not only be the center of the business but also their partner in a way as customer reviews can enhance the business or affect the brand. Artificial intelligence will play a particularly important role. Collaboration across the business will be common, and connectivity, flexibility, and rapid response will be the norm. The new business models will be a mix between digital and traditional, with a dosage of humanism and purpose. Circular economy models will continue rising to respond to the world's climate challenges and environmentally conscious customers.

No one knows for sure what the new era will be, but we know that the old business and decision-making frameworks are not applicable anymore. Businesses are obligated to be agile and have a dynamic, risk-based framework that gives them the ability to move smoothly from one plan to the next and the flexibility to respond quickly and efficiently to any disruption.

Despite all these changes, the reasons for companies to be in business will remain the same—to solve the problem or the discomfort that the customer has and to do it better than the competition. Companies should continue creating experiences for their customers and do it better than the previous time, not against or better than the competition; instead, it must be with a continuous improvement mentality. Consumers will expect more of the company each time and business need to be ready for the demand

The world will continue changing, and the resilience and adaptability to change, as well as the agility, will not be skills anymore. Rather, they will be part of our DNA and should be part of the DNA of our business.

"Live each phase, evaluate the situation, take the learnings as tools for a new approach."

Arturo Rojo-Angulo

TOOLS ————————

How can we improve decision making?

- Get out of the situation so you have a clear picture (you can reference the picture at the beginning of this chapter). Only when you are outside can you see every aspect.

- Stick to the facts; do not let emotions get involved. We have learned how our brain can be affected or manipulated by emotions.

- Always keep the purpose and the values in mind; decisions must be made based on them.

- Involve others—we are stronger and make a more informative decision when we collaborate with others.

- Do not be afraid. Sometimes you will make the wrong decision; however, it will give you a valuable lesson.

- Use the data but trust your instinct.

DECISION MAKING PROCESS

STEP 1

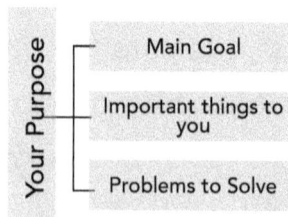

STEP 2

CRITERIA	Weighting	OPTION A		OPTION B		OPTION C	
		SCORE	TOTAL	SCORE	TOTAL	SCORE	TOTAL
TOTAL							

STEP 3

	CONSEQUENCE	PRO	CON
OPTION A			
OPTION B			
OPTION C			

Chapter 5

———

DEEP ROOT THINKING

Providing a fluid environment that harnesses change

In the previous chapters we saw that to harness change, companies need to be more agile and flexible. They need to react quickly to the customer demands and the continuous changes in the market. We also learned that to achieve this, streamlining and simplifying the process is vital. In this chapter, we will see how we need to modify the operating model or create a new model to use and adapt the new technology available. With the advances in the digital world, this is not an option or differentiation anymore; it is a necessity to survive and grow.

First, we need to understand the difference between the business model and the operating model. The business model is the company's plan for making a profit, it identifies the products or services the business plans to sell, the target market, and the cost to do it. In other words, the business model is the strategy for profitably doing business. On the other hand, the operating model describes the way the company structures the core processes. It describes how the company runs.

THE NEW OPERATING MODEL

The need for a new operating model started with the digitalization and the constant changes some years ago; however, the pandemic accelerated the necessity. The traditional operating business model was designed with a more rigid structure that conflicts with today's necessity of speed and flexibility. The specific departments, rigid chain of commands, and the interminable set of rules are an obstacle to today's requirements of technology and human connection.

Today, customers want that human relationship, they want to know how the directives of the business think, and if their lifestyle aligns with the values of the company, they want to hear and connect with the company's brand message. In the same way, employees need to feel connected and identify with the values and vision of the company. They want to have a voice, they are the ambassadors for the company, and share their opinions about the company and its products or services.

To improve the way the business operates and reacts, a new operating business model must be created for each company since the level of digitalization, technology, and artificial intelligence are different. We cannot take the trending operating model and customize it for the company as it was done before. The new operating model needs to be aligned with the company's processes, capabilities, resources, and technology. How we do it and what is needed?

The world changed, and, therefore, our way of thinking and response to the challenges must be different. We need to reinvent the business; we need to think out of the water and with a transformative and holistic vision. The philosophy of the entire model should have at the center, not only the customer and their new necessities and requirements, but also the employees, as people and their skills will be important for technology to succeed. Also, I believe that after the pandemic, what customers value will be different.

Companies are called to innovate and transform for the future; the new operating model cannot be based in the surface of the ocean, we should consider higher and deeper expectations regarding efficiency and capability, while we reduce complexity and improve cost-efficiency. Keep In mind that the goal is not to improve the existing processes with more technology or artificial intelligence, those were the goals of the past. The new goals require agility and flexibility to support and endure the fluctuations of the market and the environment.

Could you imagine what would had happen if humans believed that the only way to travel was using the automobile, and all efforts were focused on improving the existing autos and creating new models of autos? We need to re-think our business completely and use our wildest imagination to change not only the rules, but the game itself.

"Write your principles in pen and your business model in pencil."

- Josh Kopelman

NEW MODEL REQUIREMNTS

The new model must have the following requirements to be sustainable and allow growth:

- **Resilience:** The new model should give us the ability to endure any threat and change, the future remains unknown and companies should learn how to live with the uncertainty. To thrive, companies need to be able to recover critical functionality fast in any adversity and need to be able to expand or modify their capacities in a short period of time. To be resilient, companies need to embrace uncertainty and develop continuity plans that can recognize warnings and risk more rapidly and provide a detailed response with the required changes to adapt.

- **Adaptability:** These are vital requirements; it should be part of the DNA of the new operating model. The company needs to be able to modify the approach in response to a disruption. The new operative model should be built, to constantly improve and expand the company capabilities and to function within the limits. It needs to plan for the unexpected collectively. The adaptability needs to be a team effort, where all believe in their skills and capacity to endure any disruption, change, and challenge knowing that they will succeed.

- **Simple Process:** Without a simple process, the resilience and adaptability are not possible. When the complexity is reduced, companies are able to empower personnel to make decisions toward achieving business objectives. It is important in the new operating model to create a business process roadmap for continuous improvement. This map can be used to review the internal processes regularly and eliminate the not-applicable and obsolete processes. It is also important to empower the personnel to make these decisions and have clear goals and expectations. Imagine if you can have a clear holistic picture of the company's performance in a single page—a dashboard where the team can immediately understand the priorities without long meetings.

- **Collaboration:** The digitalization has improved the accessibility and the flow of information, facilitating the collaboration across teams, facilities, companies, and markets. The new operating model will encourage innovative business collaboration techniques that can improve the company's productivity by capturing the data, analyzing it, and finding trends that help with the decision making. In the era of digitalization, the connections can be internal and external, allowing the sharing of resources and skills sets for a common goal.

- **Data Analytics:** With technology providing a vast amount of data that needs to be analyzed daily, analytics is now a required capability in business. There are four primary types of data analytics:
  - Descriptive: Describe outcomes and helps answer questions about what happened.
  - Diagnostic: Identifies irregularities in the data and finds the root cause.
  - Predictive: Provides insight into what may happen in the future.
  - Prescriptive: Finds patterns in large datasets and focuses on finding the best course of action in a scenario.

- **Risk Management:** The new operating model needs to have an effective framework for risk analysis, where it is easy to identify preventable risk, the strategic risk is managed wisely, and it is well prepared to endure external risk. With the advances of technology, the new operating model needs to include technology risk and cybersecurity. The fast and hyperconnected environment of the business increases the risk outside of the company. Vendors, suppliers, and cloud providers need to be part of the risk analysis.

- **Artificial Intelligence:** The rise of artificial intelligence (AI) has transformed how people work and we see more applications used in everyday business. Customer Relationship Management (CRM) uses social data to engage with customers. Business intelligence (BI) insights originates from the data collected, analyzes them, and predicts the future. Enterprise cognitive computing (ECC) applications can automate repetitive tasks, with better accuracy and speed. The new operating model should include new AI-based operational systems to move forward and grow.

- **Ecosystems:** Since the new operating model needs to be more dynamic, the organization and structure of the business should have dynamic teams or groups with different strategic roles. In this dynamic structure, the work of each person in the ecosystem affects, and is affected by, the others. They depend on each other for survival. As in nature, these agile ecosystems should be able to adapt rapidly to any disruption and threat. These ecosystems evolve with the technology and the innovations.

- **Sustainability:** Companies are finding ways to incorporate sustainability into their products and services, and societal values into their culture to address the effect the business has in the environment and on society. The new operating model should ensure that the way we do business is addressing sustainability, making a positive impact in both areas, and is included in the strategy of the company.

- **Centralized Unified Platforms:** Digitalization started changing the operating models years ago and business operating models started moving from decentralized models with different phases of digitalization and low flexibility, to centers of excellence where digitalization was a priority and process, and technology was standardized. The new operating model should have digitalization as the core of the business with centralized and unified operating platforms that streamline the path to getting what the company and the customers need and want. Platforms simplify resources and needs with a flexible workflow environment in order to have the required agility and flexibility that customers demand.

NEW MODEL STRUCTURE

The new operating model structure needs to be fluid and simple to support the unpredictable environment. Data analysis play a vital role on the operating model, as live data will be the instrument to take decisions and offer valuable experience to the customers without compromising quality and the company's profit.

Cross functional teams are part of the new normal--operational best practices. The idea of independent departments, independent areas, and independent functions will be part of the past. Collaboration in this new model will be the key; therefore, silos should be eliminated, and regular communication should be on top of the priority list. Personnel will need to be grouped according to competencies and assigned on a project basis, to have the right combination of skills required for each project. For transformation projects it is vital that the group is formed by subject matter experts (SMEs) from the different areas to have a holistic view of the company, the capacities, and the process. This approach will minimize risks and bring a broader perspective at the same time that it provides a variety of solutions to each challenge.

The reporting structure will eventually change as well, and middle management will be either eliminated or changed to a more dynamic role. Traditional hierarchies are impacted by the rise of artificial intelligence and automation; therefore, many positions will change to different roles.

As we know, the new operating model should be more resilient and sustainable, and new technology for the same old model will not work. It needs to have an active approach that is not set in stone, it must be flexible to respond when needed and scaled well in the volatile environment.

"In order to change an existing paradigm, you do not struggle to try and change the problematic model. You create a new model and make the old one obsolete."

- Buckminster R. Fuller

The pandemic expedited the digitalization of every business and at the same time brought to the surface the process, structures, and strategies that did not apply anymore. In just months, we were able to perform the deepest SWOT Analysis ever made and see weaknesses and risks that we did not see before. Every company is in a different stage and the journey is going to be different. The phrase, "We are in the same storm, but not in the same boat," applies here. The objectives and the journey for each company are, and will continue to be, different.

The new model demands a change of skills; personnel needs to be trained for new technological jobs, they need to have better analytical skills, and a have a preventive approach with confidence in risk-taking. It also requires digital workforce solutions that help companies to automate administrative functions to create seamless workflows and support business continuity.

For the new operating business model, we need to go deep into the ocean and explore areas we never imagined. We need to be open minded, to adapt to new and creative ways to do things, and, more importantly, be confident about it. A good example is the experience I recently had with my son at an ophthalmologist visit. Every time we went, the doctor used a variety of instruments, shined bright lights directly at his eyes, and did a refraction test. The doctor then requested he look through an array of lenses to give his diagnosis. This time, the doctor was not there; instead, we had a big screen connected to a platform like zoom, from there the doctor started, asking questions while an assistant moved the equipment toward my son's eyes. The equipment transmitted the results to the doctor simultaneously. I must confess that I did not feel completely comfortable and I was annoyed that they did not inform me that the exam will be conducted this way.

On my way home, I start thinking about how innovative this idea was, and how they used technology to change their way of operating. In the past, the doctor's physical presence was only necessary to move the equipment towards people's eyes; this task can now be delegated to an assistant. Their real expertise is to diagnose after seeing the results of the test, and this can be done remotely, and thanks to the advancement in technology, it can be done simultaneously. We just need to have an open mind and embrace technology and artificial intelligence as part of our lives. If we pass the barrier, and we see the benefit they can bring to our lives, to society, and, in some cases, to the environment, we will be in a path of real transformation.

INNOVATION AND RISK

Innovation has inherent risks that can be operational, failing to meet quality, cost or demand requirements. Or, they can be financial, investing in unsuccessful innovation projects. To minimize the risk of innovation, companies should first understand the fundamental objectives to know the level of risk. Mathematician H. Igor Ansoff created matrix to understand diversification strategies. This matrix provides a rapid and simple way to think about the risks of growth and is also called the Product and Market Expansion Grid. It shows four strategies that can be used to grow, and helps to analyze the risks associated with each one. The matrix shows how each time you move into a new quadrant, either horizontally or vertically, risk increases.

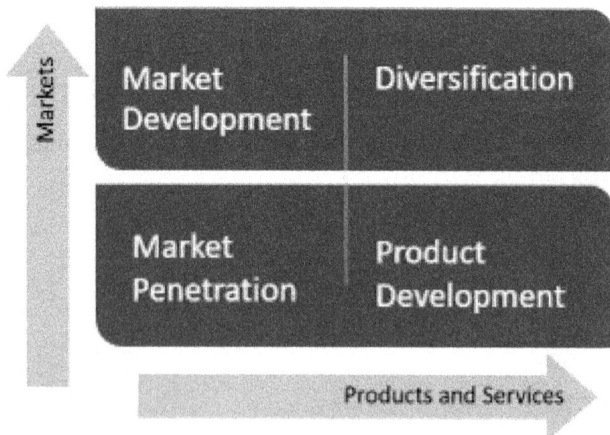

Ansoff Matrix

- **Market penetration:** This is the first quadrant on the lower left, and is the safest of the four options. The focus of this quadrant is to expand sales of the existing product in the existing market; therefore, the risk is low as you know the product and the market.

- **Product development:** This is the quadrant in the lower right; the focus of this quadrant is to introduce a new product into your existing market. Therefore, it increases the risk slightly.

- **Market development:** The quadrant in the upper left, it focuses on adding an existing product into an entirely new market, by finding a new use for the product or by adding new features or benefits to it. During the pandemic, many companies introduced their existing product into e-commerce, and the added benefit was the convenience of receiving the product at home.

- **Diversification:** The quadrant in the upper right, this focuses on introducing a new product into an entirely new market. This is the option with the higher risk because the market and the success of the product is unknown.

This matrix can be used as a framework for innovation to weigh the risks associated with several strategic and innovated options. The best way to manage the risk is to have a mix of additions to existing products or services (core) that had small risk, expand the existing business into new locations or spaces (adjacent), and transformational innovations that had the higher risk.

Companies that adopt and promote a deep innovation culture are more agile, more capable of responding to risk, and are steadier. Technology allows us to analyze vast amount of data to lower the risk as much as possible, take decisions based on good information, and manage the innovation process more efficiently. We need to keep track of the progress at each phase by using metrics and KPIs to make sure we are taking the right steps and we can react to any possible threats or disruptions.

The supply chain interruptions during the pandemic make us think about the risk to their operations that have come from pursuing cost efficiency and minimal lead times without considering the hidden cost to be paid in the event of disruption. The necessity to innovate in this area is vital. We need flexibility and a multi-level, sourcing supply chain infrastructure that eliminates the reliance we have on single-source suppliers. The cost efficiency approach is not applicable anymore and the focus on the new operating model of the supply chain must be visible in order to have an optimized structure and adaptability. Using technology to have thorough dashboards that describe the full status of procurement, production, and logistics, down to the last detail in real-time, is the innovation that every company needs to guarantee their growth.

Regardless of the rise of AI and technology, the human factor in final decision making for innovation and risk is imperative. Perhaps a modification of the Toyota's "autonomation" or automation with a human touch is the best approach here. Toyota's autonomation is a modification of the lean principle "Jidoka" that was designed to detect errors and stop a process until the problem is resolved. This principle allows a 10 to 20 percent opportunity for human expertise to make changes to improve the process. In this case, it will be to allow human intervention to make decisions on innovation when the circumstances are not clear. However, as Ben Hsieh, director of product development for Bestow, said, "In human decision-making, there can be inconsistencies and bias."

TOOL ─────────────────────────

- McKinsey's blueprint for a new operating model:

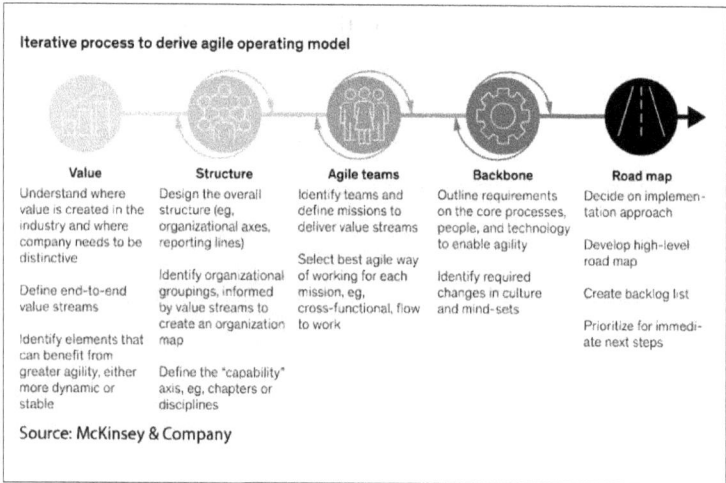

Iterative process to derive agile operating model

Value	Structure	Agile teams	Backbone	Road map
Understand where value is created in the industry and where company needs to be distinctive	Design the overall structure (eg, organizational axes, reporting lines)	Identify teams and define missions to deliver value streams	Outline requirements on the core processes, people, and technology to enable agility	Decide on implementation approach
Define end-to-end value streams	Identify organizational groupings, informed by value streams to create an organization map	Select best agile way of working for each mission, eg, cross-functional, flow to work	Identify required changes in culture and mind-sets	Develop high-level road map
Identify elements that can benefit from greater agility, either more dynamic or stable	Define the "capability" axis, eg, chapters or disciplines			Create backlog list
				Prioritize for immediate next steps

Source: McKinsey & Company

Chapter 6

EXCELLENCE

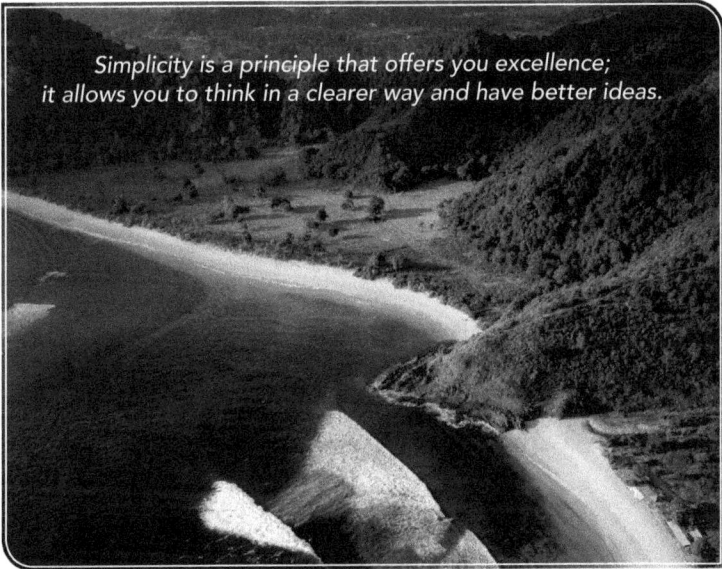

*Simplicity is a principle that offers you excellence;
it allows you to think in a clearer way and have better ideas.*

Hurricanes are like engines that require warm, moist air as fuel and wind. They form near the equator over warm ocean waters where the ocean is at least 80 degrees Fahrenheit for at least the top fifty meters below the surface. When the wind passes over the ocean's surface, water evaporates and rises. As it rises, the water vapor cools and condenses back into large water droplets, forming large clouds. Hurricanes usually weaken when they hit land because they are no longer being fed by the energy from the warm ocean waters. However, they often move far inland, dumping many inches of rain and causing lots of wind damage before they die out completely. Widespread torrential rains associated with these storms often cause flooding hundreds of miles inland. This flooding can persist for several days after a storm has dissipated.

If we think about it, the pandemic created an abrupt shift in our standard business, like a hurricane. It generated a lot of damage that will persist for months after it ends. Not all areas were affected with the same severity, but they were affected. Furthermore, many associated issues with the pandemic (torrential rains) continue causing problems to many businesses.

According to OSHA, it is important to have an evacuation plan in place to ensure that workers can get to safety in case a hurricane may affect the area. In the same way, in business, it is important that we have not only a contingency plan but a robust continuous improvement program that can ensure our business gets through any disruption.

OSHA recommends having two key elements to be prepared for these disasters, and I would like to use them as an analogy to prepare for big disruptions.

Planning

OSHA stated that a thorough plan should include:

- Conditions that will activate the plan.
- Chain of command.
- Emergency functions and who will perform them.
- Specific evacuation procedures, including routes and exits.
- Procedures for accounting for personnel, customers, and visitors.
- Equipment for personnel.

The new contingency plan for our businesses should ensure that everyone in the company knows when the contingency plan needs to be activated and who they need to contact. It is also important that employees know who is responsible for what, that employees have a specific and detailed plan for a crisis with step-by-step instructions. The plan needs to include every function in the company; previous contingency plans were designed only for operations or assume that only one area will be affected and the other areas can cover the affected one. The pandemic showed us that we need to be prepared for a complete shut down. The last thing to consider for inclusion in the plan is technology outside the normal. As we saw in 2020, almost the entire workforce went remote.

Training and Exercises

From OSHA: "Ensure that all workers know what to do in case of an emergency. Practice evacuation plans on a regular basis. Update plans and procedures based on lessons learned from exercises." The business contingency plan cannot be something that is written by someone as part of the regulatory documents and is filed somewhere only a few managers know about. The contingency plan must be known by every employee of the company and must be part of the active training. We must prepare our business for any type of disruption, not just on paper but for real.

The preparation and preventive action that a contingency plan involves is the first step to achieving operational excellence.

OPERATIONAL EXCELLENCE AND CONTINUOUS IMPROVEMENT

Operational excellence is a philosophy, a mindset

that embraces problem-solving and leadership as the key to continuous improvement. Operational excellence is when each person of the company knows the entire process flow, what the steps are, and how to get from point A to B and to C. This is not a lack of understanding and knowledge based on departments and silos. Instead, it is when every employee (who is a subject matter expert in his own field) understands the flow in other areas and, more importantly, understands how his part affects others.

Operational excellence is when the processes are simple and clear enough that anyone can have an overview of a process and get the general idea without knowing all the details. It's when every person in the company can answer basic questions about the company and its capabilities. This will only happen when the barriers and walls are down, the silos get eliminated, and the cross-training is a reality for everyone, not the luxury of a few. Operational excellence is when employees are empowered and know how to make decisions.

When we talk about operational excellence, we need to stop thinking with the old mentality of productivity, efficiency, and right the first time. Instead, we need to start looking at the big picture in a more holistic way to associate operational excellence with growth, technology, innovation, and the company's ability to sustain future operations.

"The will to win, the desire to succeed, the urge to reach your full potential... these are the keys that will unlock the door to personal excellence."

- Confucius

On the other hand, continuous improvement is ongoing improvement; it is never-ending and striving for perfection in everything. It is that path in search of excellence, a path that at our personal level implies a life that transcends, that has a purpose. We should take a step forward every day, acquiring habits or processes that are aligned with what we believe and what we want to achieve.

Continuous Improvement is the heart of many methodologies such as Lean Six Sigma, Kaizen, DMAIC, PDSA, Kanban, Gemba Walks, and Hoshin Kanri. Leveraging the right ones for our process and our company will take us to the next level.

To deploy a successful continuous improvement plan in the company, it is important that personnel is enabled to share the learnings in a methodical way. This collaboration of ideas that can come from anyone, at any time, from anywhere, creates a continuous improvement culture where everyone learns from each other.

OPERATIONAL EXCELLENCE—LEAN SIX SIGMA AND AGILE

Lean Six Sigma is a great operational excellence methodology that reduces waste and improves consistency in performance through the continuous reduction of variability in critical business processes, minimizing operating costs, and maximizing customer satisfaction. Although this methodology has been around for decades, it can be leveraged to control the chaos created by the pandemic by fomenting a culture of continuous improvement.

Agile is a more recent methodology that initiated software development and extended to multiple industries as a process for managing a project. This methodology is characterized by constant iteration and collaboration to answer the customer's needs. The Agile methodology has a fixed process structure that has proven to be beneficial in uncertain times, and it can be adapted well for remote work. The daily meetings, constant communication, and collaboration within the team promote not only the results, but it gives the regular contact that in these times is a challenge for many companies. On the other hand, the Agile teams are trained to recognize, manage, mitigate, and adapt to any risks and know how to handle unexpected changes.

Using both methodologies will take the company on the journey to excellence by providing a perfect set of tools to use in the continuous improvement plan.

CULTURAL EXCELLENCE—SHINGO GUIDING PRINCIPLES

The Shingo Guiding Principles are a good base to achieve a culture of operations excellence. Cultural transformation requires a shift in behaviors, and behaviors and culture are at the heart of the entire Shingo Model.

Shingo Guiding Principles are grouped into four areas that build a pyramid:

- **Cultural Enablers:** At the base of the pyramid
    - Respect every individual.
    - Lead with humility.
- **Drivers of Continuous Improvement:**
    - Seek Perfection.
    - Assure Quality at the Source.
    - Flow and Pull Value.
    - Embrace Scientific Thinking.
    - Focus on Process.
- **Factors That Create Alignment Across Your Organization:**
    - Think Systemically
    - Create Constancy of Purpose
- **Results:**
    - Create Value for the Customer

EXCELLENCE IN CUSTOMER SERVICE

Having great customer service is not enough anymore; customers are not looking just for a good product or a good service. They are looking for an experience and for turnkey solutions that provide analytical insights, digital excellence, and trust.

Having excellence in customer service requires partnership and trustworthiness. To achieve this, it is necessary to start with the employee--if they have access to the information and tools, and are empowered to make decisions, employees will feel motivated and change the culture of the company. These feelings will be transferred to the customer as a good experience.

Flexibility in the personnel schedules will not only be a benefit to the employee, but the customer will also have good attention the entire day. Have you ever thought about how many people would rather work different hours of the day to be able to balance their family life? The pandemic demonstrated that one of the reasons productivities increased was the ability of the remote workers to attend to their kids or other family-related activities. We know that customers do not encounter problems only from 8 to 5; therefore, if employees have a flexible schedule instead of the traditional eight-hour straight schedule, it will benefit the customer.

Technology is another key factor and should be implemented with the impact on the customer in mind, knowing that customer experience is a human experience. Provide a better experience, faster results, real-time data-driven insights, and cost-effective solutions to ensure your customers' experience is the best possible.

SUSTAINABLE EXCELLENCE

Another way to be excellent and leave a positive impact on the world is by having responsible business practices that embrace eco-efficiency and sustainability beyond the regulatory requirements. When it is done with conviction and not as an obligation, the company achieves sustainable excellence. It is also done when it creates a culture of service where the company and the employees look for ways to help and improve the social conditions of their communities. Decisions must also be made based on social and environmental impact and not only on financial gain. It is important to include and evaluate the suppliers, vendors, and other operations across the supply chains. It is no longer acceptable to ignore the impact of the company and its supply chain on the environment or the challenges of climate change.

Companies can use sustainability as a catalyst for growth and to increase innovation, and not only as a marketing strategy. In these times of continuous and rapid change, the ability to be sustainable can be a competitive advantage. Companies need to understand how to support the customer in a sustainable way and go beyond their requirements, scaling up new technologies and reducing the entire production and operation cycles. At the same time, when a company offers them innovative ideas that not only provide a solution but also help them in their sustainable journey, they are offering a customer experience that is the key to retaining the customer.

"Continuous improvement is not about the things you do well — that's work. Continuous improvement is about removing the things that get in the way of your work. The headaches, the things that slow you down, that's what continuous improvement is all about."

- Bruce Hamilton

METRICS, KPIS AND DATA ANALYTICS

Defying the metrics of the company based on the daily relevant data is imperative to strengthen the resources and to know when and what decisions to make. Identifying the right Key Performance Indicator (KPI) to track the key company functions is vital to verify if the business is operating the best it possibly can. Since times have changed, the metrics and KPIs also need to be modified to measure, evaluate, and analyze the right data.

- Metrics are meant to tell a story, to explain what happened and why. Metrics are based on historic data points.
- Key performance indicators (or KPIs) are intended to measure success and are important to track goals.
- Data analytics is used to make predictions and come to logical conclusions about future actions and decision-making. Data analytics look for the reasons and root cause of the data, therefore requiring more critical thinking skills.

Data plays an important role in the digital and volatile world we live in, and although data has been the main part of technology implementation, companies were not prepared for the abrupt disruption we all faced in 2020. Why? Simply because the data was not there. The available data was incomplete or not in real-time since the impact was global and not all suppliers and customers were on the same page digitally. Jeffrey D. Camm and Thomas H. Davenport, authors of "Data Science, Quarantine," explained the impact of the pandemic on the data. They stated: "What we're now evaluating is what happens to this accelerated, data-driven approach when a large-scale disruption, such as a global pandemic, results in a seismic shift in data. Machine learning models make predictions based on past data, but there is no recent past like today's present."

Supply chains are the most affected. Forecasting demand has always been a challenge to every company, and if you add the uncertainty of the pandemic, it is an almost impossible mission. The predictive analytics that were in high demand in the last years are not applicable anymore. The vast amount of data we used to collect is not relevant and cannot be applied to machine learning anymore. The goal now is to have data analytics platforms that can ensure the quality of the data to provide real-time insights.

With all this volatility, how can we achieve excellence? We need to start improving and simplifying the information flow, ensuring that we have the right infrastructure and framework for the applications we are using. We are walking in uncharted waters, and we need to be prepared for a day at the beach as well as hiding indoors during a hurricane.

Looking at the bright side, the data analytics solutions that in the past took months to implement are now implemented in a faster and smoother way. The goal is still the same—use data to prepare for potential scenarios and inform our decision-making. The difference now is that to achieve that excellence, data analytics must be re-invented and customized for each company situation. The model must be updated to ensure that it is aligned with the company goals and also the customer priorities and supplier's capabilities. The sources of the data need to be expanded to obtain more visibility and give power to make the right decision. It is not an easy task, but it will be rewarded. It will establish a positive, data-driven culture that will benefit the company and its employees.

SIMPLE JOURNEY TO EXCELLENCE

In this journey to excellence, we need to accelerate the shift to digital in a smart way, having innovation and simplification as the base and being vigilant of what is non-applicable. Don't replicate the complex, obsolete process, and the bad habits. We need to be intentional; we need to have clarity of our purpose and our values. When the water is turbulent, we need to deploy a sea anchor to keep us steady. The company purpose and values provide that steady steer.

To be the best, we need to build and maintain a positive work culture that motivates and empowers the employees, allowing them to become innovative, customer orientated, and continuously focused on improving themselves. It is not about the company; it is about the people—they are the ambassadors and the direct line to the customer experience. If they are respected and their opinions are valued, they will be willing to go above and beyond to achieve the goals.

The commitment to excellence should be part of every decision regarding the products or service. For that journey, we need to pack key items:

- **Integrity:** Lack of integrity is like a flood that can destroy everything.
- **Accountability:** It makes things happen.
- **Innovation:** It is part of the continuous improvement plan, and without it, the business will not survive.
- **Value to the customer:** It is not only the product or the service but in the entire relationship.

The route of that journey can be defined by the business excellence models that promote best practices, benchmarking, and tools to achieve quality and continuous improvement. The three business excellence models that are globally accepted and universally used as a baseline for other excellence models and quality awards are:

- **The Malcolm Baldrige National Quality Award (MBNQA):** It was created by the United States Commerce Department in 1987 to raise awareness of quality management in American businesses. It is based on the application of seven criteria: leadership, customer focus, strategic planning, measurement, analysis, knowledge, management, human resource focus, and performance results.

- **The European Excellence Model by EFQM:** It has an objective of helping European companies become competitive in the international marketplace, and it was built on the principles of TQMs nine criteria: leadership, people, strategy and policy, processes, partnership and resources, people results, customer results, society results, and key performance results.

- **The Deming's Prize:** Created in 1951 in acknowledgment of Dr. Edwards Deming's work in the area of industrial quality control. It is the oldest award, and it has four categories: The Deming Prize for Individuals, the Deming Distinguished Service Award for Dissemination and Promotion, the Deming Application Prize, and the Quality Control Award for Operating Business Units.

MY WISH FOR YOU

We are underwater. Nevertheless, we are in an interesting and unexplored journey, and it is our decision what we do and how we react. Oceans are powerful, and full of challenges and adventures. If we learn what tools we need to use for each specific time and day, we can enjoy the magic within.

A surfboard for days on the beach, a snorkel for the times that need a little more investigation and study, scuba gear for that deep diving into the process and transformations, and full gear in case of a hurricane.

My wish for you is that today you decide to start the exploration to increase your understanding of the company. This exploration can reveal if the company is managed effectively, is sustainable, and if the resources are properly allocated.

Take an opportunity to look at your business,

dissecting each area, each process, each structure, and see what tools you need to use. Do not be afraid to dive deeper and discover what external and internal sources are affecting your company and how. And when you get to the deep ocean, where the light begins to fade and the pressure is intense, remember that the knowledge you are acquiring along with this ridiculously simple process enables you to thrive in any extreme and disruptive conditions.

"Bringing the processes to a ridiculously simple version could be the only way to survive in this disruptive market."

Adriana Rosso-Angulo

AUTHOR BIOGRAPHY

Adriana Rozo-Angulo is a passionate leader, strategist, and change agent. She is the Director of Operations at Menasha and is currently working with the Business Transformation team. Adriana is also the President of MAS Connections, a business consultancy firm she co-found in 2011. Adriana is a Lean Six Sigma Black Belt professional and holds several certifications in the manufacturing and medical device industry.

During her twenty years in the industry, Adriana realized that one of the main factors that affect companies of any size are the "Not Applicable" processes, ideas, and mindset. Her strategic and operational expertise, combined with her lean six sigma background, allow her to promptly identify these situations and create a simpler and sustainable strategy.

Adriana is the New Jersey Hub Leader for The Hispanic Star, an organization under We Are All Human. She is a member of the Advisory Board of Seton Hall University for the "Transformative Leadership in Disruptive Times" executive certificate program. Adriana is also a certified EXMA speaker and co-author of the book *Hispanic Star Rising*.